LEARN
Tree
and the Fizzy Lemonade

Once upon a moment, not so long ago
A little seed fell on to some soft ground
It felt so good that he snuggled
underneath an old brown leaf
And went fast to sleep.

In the morning, Sun climbed out
from behind a hill, and said,

"Little seed it's time to grow
I'll teach you all there is to know
Listen well and you will be
The one they call the Learning Tree."

. . . and Seed stretched out his arms and
grew . . . And Grew . . . AND GREW.

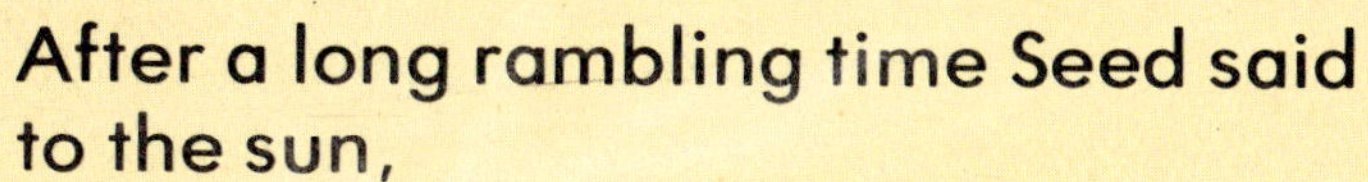

After a long rambling time Seed said
to the sun,
"I have listened and I have grown
Am I now the tree you said I'd be?"

"You are indeed," said the sun,

"The Learning Tree."

It was a bright sunny morning when Timothy and Emma made their way up the hill to see Learning Tree. Emma had brought a bottle of fizzy lemonade and every so often she would stop and suck a little through a stripy green straw.

"Come on," said Tim, "if you keep stopping we'll never get there."

Emma really didn't care. She would have been quite content to drink lemonade all day.

By the time the children reached the pond, Emma had drunk so much fizzy lemonade that she felt as if her tummy was going to burst. She offered Timothy the rest, but he just wasn't thirsty. Emma couldn't drink another drop, so with a fizzy sigh she poured it into the pond. At that moment a voice bellowed down the hill.

"Fish have feelings, you know." It was the Learning Tree.

"What do you mean?" enquired Tim.

"I mean," said Learning Tree crossly, "that there are fish living in that pond and they certainly don't like fizzy lemonade poured into their water."

The tree pointed a leaf at Emma. "Now, what have you got to say for yourself young lady?"
Emma had nothing to say for herself.

"Don't be cross with her," pleaded Tim. "I'm sure she didn't mean to pour lemonade over the fish."

Emma suddenly saw the funny side of things and began to giggle.

"There," snapped the tree, "she thinks it's funny now! How would she like it if someone poured lemonade over her?"

"That would be funny," laughed Em.
"Funny eh!" exclaimed Learning Tree.

Emma's smile disappeared as the tree chanted some magic words.

"Winds that blow 'cross hill and glade
Send some fizzy lemonade
Pour it down upon Em's head
So she'll remember what I said."

Suddenly, from nowhere in particular, a large lemonade bottle appeared. It floated over Emma's head and poured its fizzy contents all over her. The bubbles crept up her nose and her hair was quite sticky. She was in a mess!

"You horrible tree!" she screamed.

Now it was Learning Tree's turn to giggle. "How does that feel?" he laughed.

"You've made me very cross," said Emma.

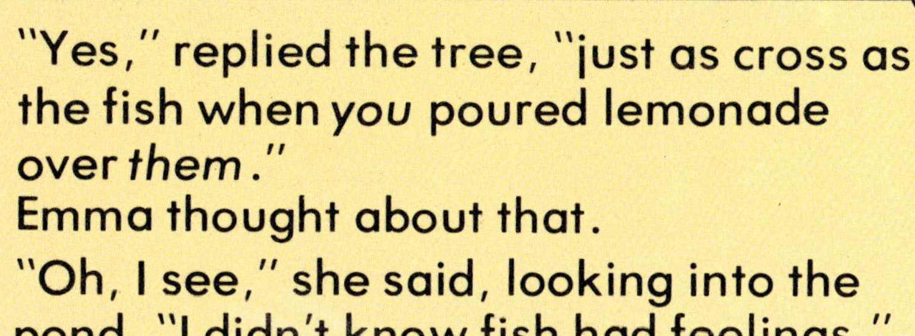

"Yes," replied the tree, "just as cross as the fish when *you* poured lemonade over *them*."

Emma thought about that.

"Oh, I see," she said, looking into the pond. "I didn't know fish had feelings."

The fish in the pond certainly did have feelings.

Their fins turned red with rage and they swam to and fro blowing the most enormous bubbles.

"Will they be all right?" asked Tim.
"They will this time," replied Learning Tree, "but could you imagine what would happen if everyone who passed by poured lemonade and things like that into the pond? My goodness, the fish would get very ill and soon there'd be none left."

Emma was horrified.
"I shall never pour lemonade in the pond again," she said.

Tim suddenly had an awful thought. "If Emma goes home covered in lemonade I don't think her mother will be very pleased," he said.

"Don't worry, I'll clean her up with some magic," replied Learning Tree.

"Now Emma, I want you to turn around three times."
Emma turned around three times and disappeared.
"Oh dear!" said the tree crossly, "it must have been four times!"

Learning Tree closed his eyes and thought very hard. He thought so hard that his branches began to tremble with the effort.

"I've got it," he said, "by Rumplestiltskin's magic eye, bring Em back all clean and dry."

Emma appeared in a wisp of smoke and bubbles. She was quite clean and dry.

"Sorry about that," said Learning Tree. "That's all right," replied Em, "your magic really worked."

Emma had appeared just in time, for Timothy heard his mother calling the children in for tea.

"We've got to go now," said Tim, "but we'll see you tomorrow."

Emma put her empty lemonade bottle in the rubbish bin and the children went home for tea. After that day Timothy and Emma were always very careful to keep the water in the pond fresh and clean, thanks to Learning Tree, of course.

FISH HAVE FEELINGS

Fish have feelings yes they do
They can be happy just like you
When they're sad they cry a tear
And fishes get scared if you go too near

Fish have feelings yes they do
They can be grumpy just like you
They're not fond of lemonade
Oh wait 'till you see the mess you've made

Every fish must have one thing
On water they depend
So keep it clean bright and clear
And you will be their friend

Fish have feelings, yes they do
They can be jolly just like you
If you listen hard and long
You might even hear them sing this song

Every time you see a pond
A river or a stream
Remember what the fishes say
Please keep our water clean

Fish have feelings yes they do
Make a funny face and they'll laugh at you
Fish have feelings some are shy
Aren't they a bit like you and I?

The End